The Workbook To:

'If Only Someone Would Listen To What I Have To Say'

- Learn basic money principles
- Learn where money comes from
- Practice saving techniques
- Learn how your dreams can help get you to your goals
- Learn how to use the 'Rule of 10'
- Learn about banking and checking accounts

Written by Donna Rosby © 2018

ACKNOWLEDGEMENTS

This is a publication of Donna Rosby

Thank you to my family and friends for encouraging me to move forward with my passion to educate and inform our youth. Thank you to God for giving me the vision to design this workbook in a way that was given to me in my dreams. Thank you to the children that will learn to dream and grow from this book.

Thank you to my editor, for his valuable contributions to the editing, formatting, and insight to the book and the workbook.

Copyright 2018 by Donna Rosby MBA, BS, RN

All rights reserved. No part of this book may be reproduced, resold, or transmitted in any form or by any means, by photostat, photocopying, recording, microfilm, xerography, or any other means, or incorporated into any information storage and retrieval system, electronic or mechanical, without the written permission of the copyright owner.

You may contact:

Donna Rosby

@MiKash Corporation http://www.mikash.net Donna@mikash.net

ISBN-13: 978-1727595352

ISBN-10: 1727595351

Printed in the USA

Thank You To My Readers of:

'If Only Someone Would Listen To What I Have To Say '

(written by Donna Rosby)

I believe that knowledge is power and action brings knowledge to life.

By learning BASIC money principles, you will be prepared to manage your money before entering college and be ready for the money challenges faced by adults every day.

Thank you for the opportunity to show you a simple way to look at money differently and for opening your mind to learning something new.

Minimal Requirements

Some things needed throughout this workbook process:

- Pencil and a journal (small or large)
- Piggy bank of any kind (can be a jar, box, anything to hold money)
- Bring an open mind
- $1.00
- Parents approval

THIS KIDS MONEY WORKBOOK BELONGS TO

_____

Table of Contents

Introduction 7
Dream Again 8
How to Capture Your Dream... 12
Write Your Dreams 14
Where Does Money Come From 16
The Face of The Dollar Bill.. 21
What Money Can't Buy... 24
The 'Rule of 10'..27
"How Opportunity Cost Can Change Your Way of Thinking" 31
Terms You Should Know...35

Introduction

The goal of this workbook:

To educate you on how to start thinking differently about money and to help you learn why journaling can be helpful to the process encouraging you to start journaling.

If you take the concepts taught in this book seriously, they could eventually lead you down the road to financial freedom, whatever that may mean to you.

Chapter 2

Dream Again

Why is Dreaming So Important?

Do you remember when you were a small child and had to find things to do with your time?

How about making up new things to do with your old toys?

Did you dream about what you wanted to be when you grew up?

Did you imagine yourself being somewhere else when you got in trouble?

Do you remember when your imagination was vivid and wild?

That was your imagination at its peaking point. There were no filters to stop you from thinking the unthinkable. You were like superman or superwoman. You could travel to the moon, or become a doctor, a nurse, a lawyer; anything you wanted. The sky was the limit because there was no one who told you that you couldn't.

As you age, life happens, barriers arrive, and negative & competitive people come into your life. Sometimes, you let your fears get in the way of your dreaming.

This workbook will help you to start dreaming again allowing you to unleash the desires of your heart and discovering how to fund that dream with money you've learned to save.

As you learn to dream again, these dreams can open the door to your purpose in life. Once you know your purpose, how do you fund that purpose?

Wouldn't that be great to know what you were put here for?

Wouldn't it be great to know what you want to do with your life when you grow up?

It can happen!

NOW, If you know what you want to do, wouldn't it be amazing if you had the money to do it?

Wouldn't that be fantastic?

By learning the basic financial principles in this book, such as how to make save, manage, and invest money, you can be 10 steps ahead of everyone else.

The *'Rule of 10'* is your start to financial freedom.

Now lets do this!!!!!!!!!!!!!!!!!

Chapter 3

How To Capture Your Dream

How to Capture Your Dream

1. Use the bathroom before going to bed- this prevents breaking the dream cycle.
2. Write your thoughts for the day down before you go to bed.
3. Write your thoughts when you wake up.
4. Write whatever thoughts wake you up at night or you remember when you wake.
5. WRITE the last dream you can remember on the next page.

Don't wait, don't think about it...Just write it

Keep a journal at your bedside and on you at all times!!!!

WRITE YOUR LAST DREAM

Chapter 4

Write Your Dreams

WRITE YOUR PAST DREAMS

Chapter 5

Where Does Money Come From

Where Does Money Come From
Money moves in a circle

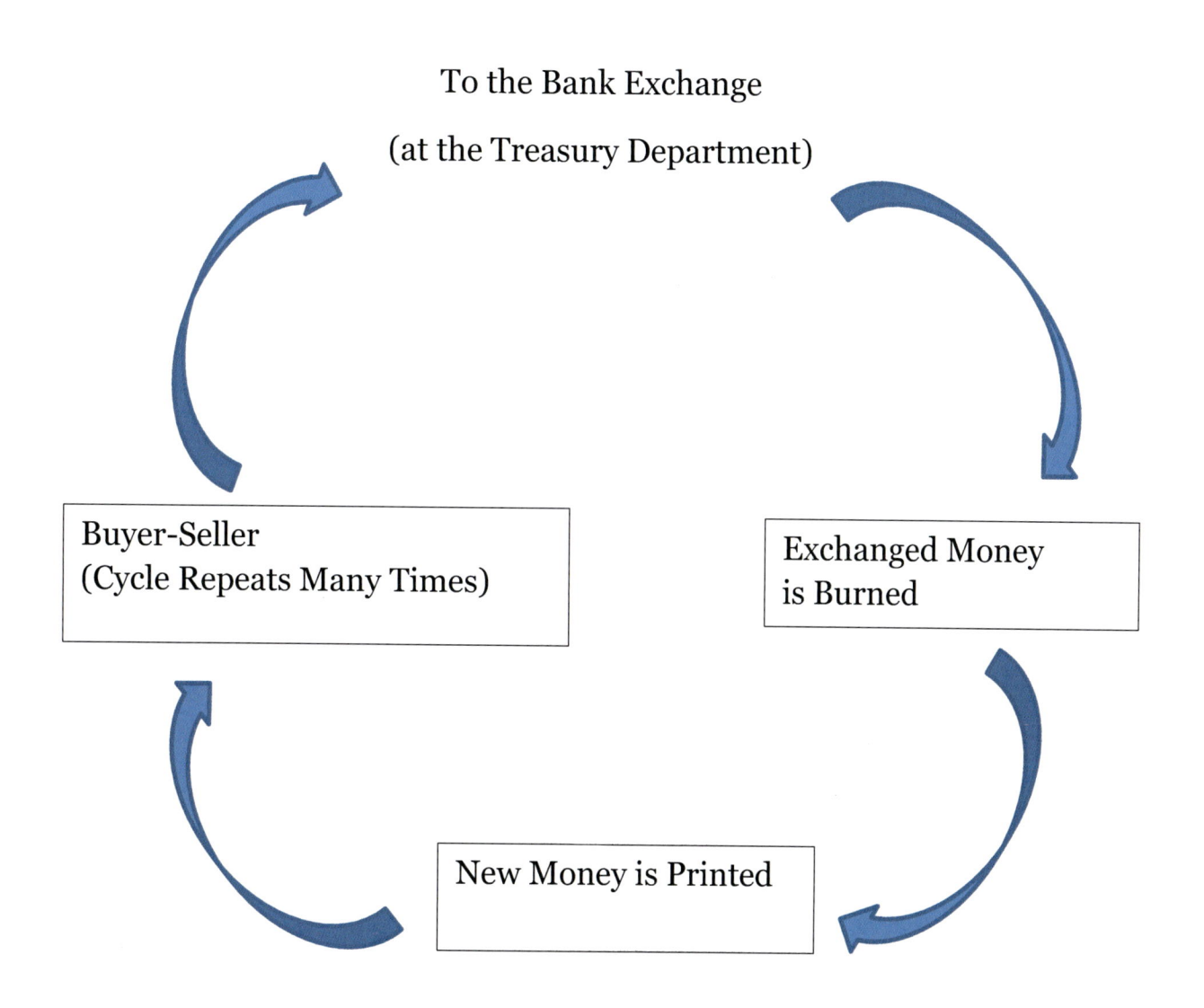

To the Bank Exchange

(at the Treasury Department)

- Buyer-Seller (Cycle Repeats Many Times)
- Exchanged Money is Burned
- New Money is Printed

A Little Money History

"1792 Congress passed into law the dollar money system"

1. The original currency was silver and gold.
2. 1913 The Federal Reserve System evolved.
3. They regulate the supply of money so that the country can grow economically.
4. Currently, our currency are bills and coins.

What products do we use with the remains of burned money (circle all that apply)

A. Candy

B. Roofing material

C. Clothes

D. Insulation

E. Cars

F. Food

See Page 42 for the answers

Chapter 6

The Face of The Dollar Bill

The faces of the dollar bill

Each bill has its own special ink on a special kind of paper to help prevent counterfeit

Presidents are the faces of the front of the bills:

- One dollar bill is George Washington
- Two dollar bill is Thomas Jefferson
- Five dollar bill is Abraham Lincoln
- Ten dollar bill is Alexander Hamilton
- Twenty dollar bill is Andrew Jackson
- Fifty dollar bill is Ulysses Grant
- One hundred dollar bill is Benjamin Franklin

Assign the president to its correlating dollar bill

$10.00   George Washington

$50.00   Abraham Lincoln

$2.00   Benjamin Franklin

$1.00   Thomas Jefferson

$20.00   Ulysses Grant

$5.00   Alexander Hamilton

$100.00   Andrew Jackson

(Answer on page 42)

Chapter 7

What Money Can't Buy

What Money Can't Buy

As the discussion of money continues REMEMBER, money can't buy everything.

Write down 4 things that money can't buy:

1. _____
2. _____
3. _____
4. _____

Savings

You Can Do It

Chapter 8

The 'Rule of 10'

'The Rule of 10'

"10% of everything you own is yours to keep"

-The richest man in Babylon

- Put 10% of your money in a safe place for fun-NOW MONEY
- Put 10% of your money in savings- SHORT TERM MONEY
- Put 10% of your money in an investment account-LONG-TERM
- Put the rest of your money in a youth account for everything else you may need

How To Implement the Savings Plan

NOW

- Use this money for anything/anytime
- You can share or help others

SHORT-TERM

- Use for large purchases
- Save up over short period of time for something you really want

LONG-TERM

- Money in the bank
- DON'T TOUCH THIS MONEY
- Add to it and watch it grow
- Investment account included

Write Down What You Are Going To Do With Your Next Allowance

1. _____
2. _____
3. _____
4. _____
5. _____
6. _____
7. _____
8. _____
9. _____
10. _____
11. _____
12. _____
13. _____

Chapter 9

"How Opportunity Cost Can Change Your Way of Thinking"

What is Opportunity Cost

- ❖ Money itself has no value
- ❖ Understand that money represents VALUE
- ❖ Money represents the value of other things that we can get with it

Knowing that:

<u>Opportunity Cost is what you sacrifice when you buy something else</u>

For example: If you buy those shoes (A), you sacrifice the opportunity to buy that outfit (B)

Therefore, choose slowly when buying, take your time, check for lower prices, shop around.

Write down 5 things in your room that you would trade for something else if you needed cash

Ex. New clothes   vs   Lightly Used Clothes

1. _____ vs _____
2. _____ vs _____
3. _____ vs _____
4. _____ vs _____
5. _____ vs _____

You have completed your 1st opportunity cost lesson....

FANTASTIC.........

Now, tell a friend

Quotes To Help You Get Ready For Your Future

Before you speak, listen. Before you write, think. Before you spend, earn. Before you invest, investigate. Before you criticize, wait. Before you pray, forgive. Before you quit, try. Before you retire, save. Before you die, give.

    -William A. Ward

If you don't want to work, you have to earn enough money so that you won't have to work.

    -Ogden Nash

There is no friend as loyal as a book.

    -Ernest Hemingway

Chapter 10

Terms You Should Know

Terms to Know

Profit - The money a company makes from selling its products

Federal Reserve - National banking system in charge of the money supply in the US

Fiduciary - A person who takes care of money for other people

Stocks - Shares of a company that you can buy

Investment - The action of investing money for a profit

Compound Interest - Interest paid on top of the interest daily instead on once/yr.

Risk - The possibility that you'll lose money when investing

TO DO LIST

- ❏ Make a needs list (what do you need today to start)

- ❏ Ask parents for allowance and ways to earn more

- ❏ Buy 3 savings jars & label

    - *Now, Short-term, Long-term*

- ❏ Open bank accounts (checking and savings)

- ❏ Open an investment account (with parents)

- ❏ Look at all bills with presidents

(1,2,5,10,20,50,100 dollar bill- online for larger bills)

Learn them!

- ❏ Write down ways to make extra money

- ❏ Sell something, do a job- clean the kitchen, mow the lawn, yard-sale, collect cans, etc.

- ❏ After you list, pick one job and start it now…

- ❏ Tell your friends what you're doing, see who else wants to join you

Notes For Your To Do List

List 6 new ways to make money

1. _____
2. _____
3. _____
4. _____
5. _____
6. _____

Bank Account Information

(KEEP IN A SAFE PLACE AT ALL TIMES)

Name of bank: _____

Address of bank: _____

Bank phone Number: _____

Checking Account Number: _____

Savings Account Number: _____

Investment Account Name: _____

Investment Account Number: _____

To accomplish great things, we must not only act, but also dream; not only plan, but also believe.

-Anatole France

ANSWER KEY

Page 20: What products do we use ...

Answer:

*   ROOFING MATERIALS

*   INSULATION

Page 23: Assign the president ...

Answer:

$10.00	Alexander Hamilton
$50.00	Ulysses Grant
$2.00	Thomas Jefferson
$1.00	George Washington
$20.00	Andrew Jackson
$5.00	Abraham Lincoln
$100.00	Benjamin Franklin

Made in the USA
Columbia, SC
25 November 2021